DATE DUE

Bow
Wow

Kelly Doudna

Consulting Editor, Monica Marx, M.A./Reading Specialist

Published by SandCastle™, an imprint of ABDO Publishing Company, 4940 Viking Drive, Edina, Minnesota 55435.

Printed in the United States.

Credits
Edited by: Pam Price
Curriculum Coordinator: Nancy Tuminelly
Cover and Interior Design and Production: Mighty Media
Photo Credits: Digital Vision, Kelly Doudna, Hemera

Library of Congress Cataloging-in-Publication Data

Doudna, Kelly, 1963-
    Bow wow / Kelly Doudna.
        p. cm. -- (Sound words)
    Includes index.
    Summary: Uses photographs and simple sentences to introduce words for different sounds that animals make. Includes a short story using some of these words.
    ISBN 1-59197-450-X
    1. English language--Onomatopoeic words--Juvenile literature. 2. Sounds, Words for--Juvenile literature. [1. Animal sounds. 2. English language--Onomatopoeic words. 3. Sounds, Words for.] I. Title.

PE1597.D63 2003
428.1--dc21

2003044345

SandCastle™ books are created by a professional team of educators, reading specialists, and content developers around five essential components that include phonemic awareness, phonics, vocabulary, text comprehension, and fluency. All books are written, reviewed, and leveled for guided reading, early intervention reading, and Accelerated Reader® programs and designed for use in shared, guided, and independent reading and writing activities to support a balanced approach to literacy instruction.

Let Us Know

After reading the book, SandCastle would like you to tell us your stories about reading. What is your favorite page? Was there something hard that you needed help with? Share the ups and downs of learning to read. We want to hear from you! To get posted on the ABDO Publishing Company Web site, send us e-mail at:

sandcastle@abdopub.com

SandCastle Level: Transitional

Onomatopoeia

(on-uh-mat-uh-**pee**-uh) is the use of words that sound like what they describe.

These **sound words** are all around us.

Ducks waddle around
the farm.

Quack!

The dog plays with
a bone.

Woof!

The rooster sits in the yard.

Cock-a-doodle-doo!

The cat is hungry.

Meow!

The sheep walks in the field.

Baa!

The cow eats grass.

Moo!

Harry the horse trots around
the farm, clip clop, clip clop.

He greets Greg the goose
and Robby the rooster.

16

"Whinny!" neighs Harry.

"Cock-a-doodle-doo!" crows Robby.

"Honk!" hollers Greg.

17

Harry trots by the house.

"Woof!" barks Dave the dog.

"Meow!" mews Cathy the cat.

Harry trots to the field.

"Moo!" croons Cody the cow.

"Baa!" bleats Sherry the sheep.

19

Harry trots to the barn.

"Hee haw!" brays Don
the donkey.

"Oink!" squeals Peggy the pig.

Harry hurries to his stall.

"I've said hi to all my friends!"

Picture Index

baa, pp. 13, 19

meow, pp. 11, 18

moo, pp. 15, 19

oink, p. 20

quack, p. 5

woof, pp. 7, 18

Glossary

barn   a building on a farm where animals are kept

farm   land used for raising animals or growing crops

field   the open fenced-in farmland where animals graze or crops are grown

stall   a small area in a stable or barn where a single animal, such as a horse, is kept

trot   a brisk pace that is faster than a walk

waddle   to sway from side to side while taking short steps

About SandCastle™

A professional team of educators, reading specialists, and content developers created the SandCastle™ series to support young readers as they develop reading skills and strategies and increase their general knowledge. The SandCastle™ series has four levels that correspond to early literacy development in young children. The levels are provided to help teachers and parents select the appropriate books for young readers.

Emerging Readers
(no flags)

Beginning Readers
(1 flag)

Transitional Readers
(2 flags)

Fluent Readers
(3 flags)

These levels are meant only as a guide. All levels are subject to change.

To see a complete list of SandCastle™ books and other nonfiction titles from ABDO Publishing Company, visit **www.abdopub.com** or contact us at:

4940 Viking Drive, Edina, Minnesota 55435 • 1-800-800-1312 • fax: 1-952-831-1632